RESOURCE GUIDE

PLAY and PLAY

Teaching Kids to Play the Piano

Written by Diane Engle

© 2020 by Diane Engle
All rights reserved.
Song Sheets Appendix pages 34-48 may be reproduced by the purchaser of this book. No other part of this book may be reproduced in any form or by any electronic or mechanical means, including information storage and retrieval systems, without permission in writing from the author.

dianeengle52@gmail.com
Diane Engle
107 S. Holly Street
DeQuincy, LA 70633
USA

www.dianeenglepianostudio.com

Illustrator: Peggy Condon
Pre-Press Production: Julie Karen Hodgins

CONTENTS

Introduction 3
Piano Summer Camp 4
Lesson Plan for Piano Summer Camps 6
    Day One 6
    Day Two 15
    Day Three 19
    Day Four 22
    Day Five 24
Current/Returning Students Piano Camp 28
Operating a Profitable Year Round Piano Studio 29
Song Sheets Appendix 34

INTRODUCTION

How do I have a profitable piano studio in a small town, population 3,200? Two principal ways:

1. I teach in **small groups**, teaching three days a week, 12 hours per week.
2. I hold **Piano Summer Camps** to recruit new students as well as to retain current students.

This book will teach you how to have a profitable piano studio wherever you are located. Here is what you will find:

- Piano Summer Camp recruitment schedule.
- Detailed lesson plans for a 5-day piano camp for young beginners.
- Reproducible song sheets for students. Every song sheet is also a color sheet and a game song.
- Specific instructions for setting up a piano studio for teaching in small groups.
- Supplemental information about piano summer camp for current/returning students.

I have followed the lesson plans for the piano camp for young beginners exactly as it's written in this book. I know it can work for you.
You will have fun teaching!

Diane Engle

PIANO SUMMER CAMP

ADVERTISING AND RECRUITING
Here is the schedule for advertising and recruiting new students:
- Advertise 3 to 4 months in advance.
- Advertise on social media, in the local newspaper, and in the local neighborhood paper.
- Ad should include:
  - **PIANO SUMMER CAMP**, *a fun way to jumpstart piano lessons for beginners!* Or *an introduction to piano in a fun setting!*
  - Dates of the camp.
  - Session Times: Examples- 1:00-3:00 p.m.; 3:00-5:00 p.m.
  - Location.
  - Tuition Cost, which should include all materials and snacks. Suggestion for tuition cost - charge what is two times the **monthly** tuition charge in your area for 1 day a week piano lessons. Be sure to factor in the costs of materials and snacks.
  - Your contact information, both phone and email.

REGISTERING STUDENTS
Register students via an online enrollment application. I developed one from the *Contact Information Form* found in *Document Forms* of Google Drive. The enrollment application should include:

- Email address
- Student's name and age
- Parent(s) name and phone number
- Mailing address
- Emergency contact name and phone number
- List of any food allergies
- Permission for social media photos and newspaper photos

FOLLOW-UP PROCEDURES
After parents have submitted the application, follow up with these things:

- Email parents, listing detailed information about the camp:
    - Date, time, and location.
    - Tuition amount and when it is due.
    - A message that tells them they will be receiving an email reminder one week prior to the camp and that their child will be receiving a personal letter from you.

- One week before camp:
    - Mail a personal letter to each student along with a business card with date and time of the camp.
    - Email reminder to parents.

- Text reminder or call parents the day before camp begins.

All of the procedures will set you up to have a successful piano camp.
Now, let's get started!

There is a keyboard for each student as they use the PLAY AND PLAY piano book.

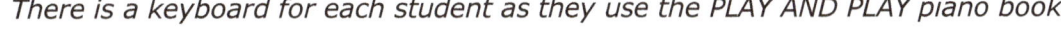

LESSON PLANS

These lesson plans are formatted for a 5-day piano camp, 2 hour sessions per day.

DAY ONE

A. OBJECTIVES. The students will:
   1. Develop a feeling of the steady beat.
   2. Develop an understanding of the 5 finger numbers.
   3. Develop an understanding of the black key groups.

B. MATERIALS
   1. Bee puppet or picture
   2. Tambourine or drum
   3. Snail puppet or picture
   4. Ball
   5. Small wallet or picture
   6. Blank paper for students to trace their hands.

C. PROCEDURES
   1. Greeting
      a. Teacher introduces himself/herself.
      b. Bee story and **BEE, BEE, BUMBLEBEE** poem.

Hold Bee and say, "Bee wants to meet everyone just like you met me." Say the poem, tapping your head lightly with the bee on the steady beat.

c. On the last word, *out*, say, "The bee landed on my head on the word *out*. That means he met me and now I am out of the group. I will help Bumblebee move around the room to meet someone else." Walk around the room, touch objects in the room and each student's head with a steady beat as you say the poem. Be sure to land on a student's head on the last word of the poem and say, "Bee wants to know your name." Then that student walks with you, helping to hold the bee and to land on another student on the word *out*.
The game continues until every student has had a turn to hold the bee and say the poem. The last student should land on the teacher's head at the end of the poem.

BEE, BEE, BUMBLE BEE

2. FINGER NUMBERS
    a. "Before we begin playing the piano, we need to learn our finger names. Just like each one of us has a name, our fingers have a number name."
    b. Hold up both hands, wiggle each finger and say the numbers. Be sure to name thumb as finger 1.
    c. Students hold up hands, count fingers 1-5, wiggling each finger as they count.
    d. Students wiggle the finger that you call out in random order.
    e. Have students trace hands and number their fingers on a blank piece of paper.
    f. Tell the students that it's time to use their finger numbers to play the piano/keyboard.

3. BLACK KEYS, page 35
   a. Guide the students to identify and play the black keys as shown in the teacher instructions below.
   b. Students will follow instructions as found on student worksheet.

PIANO KEYBOARD

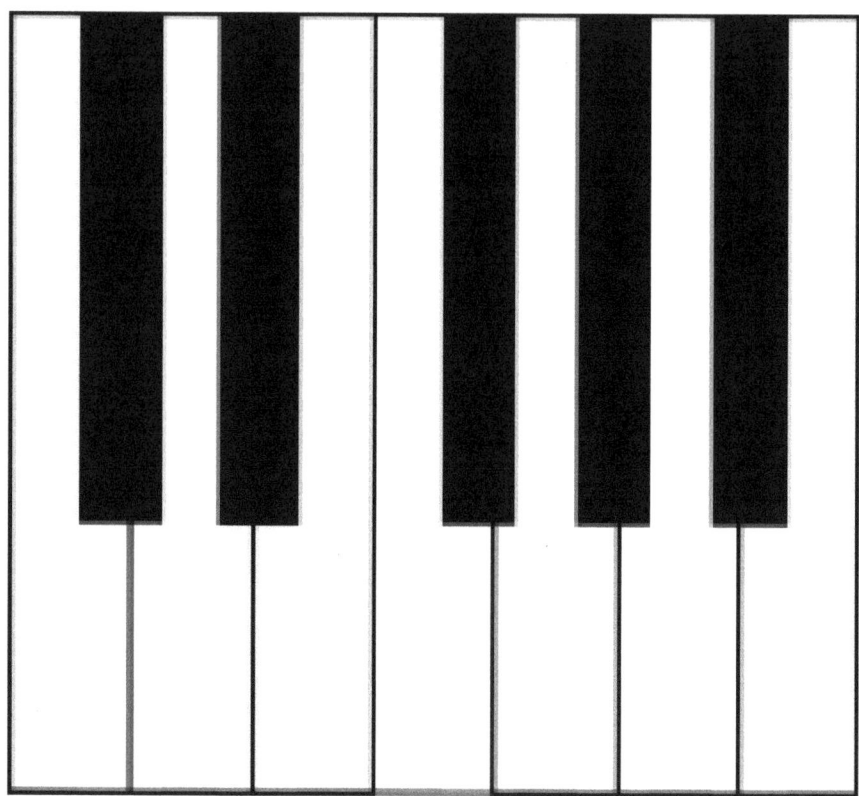

(page 10 *PLAY AND PLAY* Teacher Edition)

KEYBOARD

TEACHER INSTRUCTIONS

Demonstrate the correct finger and hand position: fingers curved, fingertips on the keys, wrist straight, arms bent at a right angle at the elbow.

BLACK KEY GROUPS: TWO BLACK KEYS

1. Instruct students to look at the black keys and notice the black keys are in different groups. Ask, "How many black keys are in a group?"
2. Instruct students to circle the group of two black keys on the page.
3. Model playing all of the groups of two black keys using fingers 2 and 3 of both hands.
4. Instruct students to follow your model and use fingers 2 and 3 of both hands to play all of the groups of two black keys. They will start with the left hand then change to the right hand when they get to the middle of the keyboard.

BLACK KEY GROUPS: THREE BLACK KEYS

1. Instruct students to circle the group of three black keys on the page.
2. Model playing all of the groups of three black keys using fingers 2, 3, and 4 of both hands.
3. Instruct students to follow your model and use fingers 2, 3, and 4 of both hands to play all of the groups of three black keys. They will start with the left hand then change to the right hand when they get to the middle of the keyboard.

Transition: Tell the students that it's time to learn a game song to play using the black keys. They will learn the singing game first.

4. *SNAIL, SNAIL,* page 36

    a. Sing the song. Students echo.
    b. Students play the game as instructed below.
    c. Students play the song on the piano/keyboard.

TEACHER INSTRUCTIONS
Sing the song and play the game before introducing the song on the piano/keyboard.

GAME INSTRUCTIONS
Story: *Snails love the flower garden. They also love the rain because the rain makes the flowers grow. Let's pretend we are the snail in the garden and we are going 'round and 'round.*
CIRCLE GAME: Teacher and students join hands to walk in a circle as they sing.
SNAIL SHELL GAME: Teacher and students join hands to form a straight line. The teacher is the line leader. The student at the end of the line stands still as the teacher leads the line around the student to wind the line into the snail shell.

PIANO / KEYBOARD INSTRUCTIONS
Students place left hand on a group of 2 black keys and right hand on a group of 3 black keys. Guide the students to play with right hand when finger number 2 is above the picture and with left hand when finger 2 is below the picture.

    d. Students color the pictures as you work with individual students as the piano/keyboard.

5. *IN AND OUT*, page 37

In and out, 'round a-bout, O U T and that spells out!

    a. Sing the song as the students listen. Pass a beanbag back and forth between your hands as you sing. Tell the students you are staying steady as you pass the beanbag back and forth. Refer to the steady beat as "heartbeat."
    b. Students play the game as instructed.
    c. Students play the song on the piano/keyboard.
    d. Students color the bean bag pictures as you work with individual students at the piano/keyboard.

TEACHER INSTRUCTIONS
Play the game before introducing the song on the piano/keyboard.

GAME INSTRUCTIONS
Objects Needed
- Beanbag for passing on the steady beat.
- Rhythm sticks
- Hand drum

Students stand in a circle and pass the beanbag around the circle. The person who has the beanbag on the last word of the song, *"out", is out of the circle.* Send the person who is out to one of the rhythm instruments to keep the steady beat as the game continues.

PIANO/KEYBOARD INSTRUCTIONS
Review the groups of two and three black keys. Students place left hand on a group of two black keys and right hand on a group of three black keys. Guide the students to play with right hand when the finger number 2 is high above the bean bag picture and with left hand when finger number 2 is below the bean bag picture. The students will nod their head for the silent heartbeat on lines 1, 2, and 4.

6. BREAK-Snack Time 15 minutes. Suggested snacks for the camp include lemonade and cookies, popsicles, or ice cream.

Students are playing the game song, "CLOSET KEY".

7. HEARTBEAT CHART, p. 38

8. *APPLE, PEACH, PEAR, PLUM*

a. Say the poem as you stand in front of a student and pat the steady beat on the tambourine or drum
b. Student tells his/her birthday at the end of the poem.
c. Repeat the poem until all students have told their birthday.
d. Students say the poem with the teacher, patting the steady beat / heartbeat with both hands on their lap as you play the beat on the instrument.
e. Teacher demonstrates keeping the steady beat by touching each heart on the HEARTBEAT CHART, while saying the poem.
f. Students touch the HEARTBEAT CHART and say the poem while you play the instrument with one hand and touch the chart with the other. Instruct the students that each time they touch a heart it should match when the instrument is played.
g. Each student has a turn to play the instrument as the other students touch the heartbeat pictures.

PLAY AND PLAY - one student plays the game song, "BOUNCE HIGH" on the keyboard as another student plays the game.

9. *BOUNCE HIGH,* 39

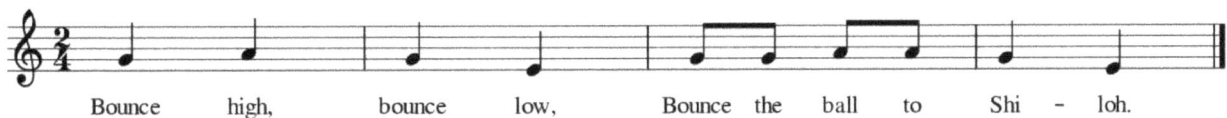

a. Sing the song. Students echo.
b. Students play the game as instructed.
c. Students play the song on the piano.
d. Students color the pictures as the teacher works with individual students at the piano/keyboard.

BOUNCE HIGH

TEACHER INSTRUCTIONS
Sing the song and play the game before the students play the music on the piano/keyboard.

GAME DIRECTIONS
Object Needed
- Large Ball

Students stand in a circle. Teacher stands in the middle of the circle and bounces the ball to each child as the song is sung. Student bounces the ball back to the teacher.

Variations:
- Students bounce the ball to next student around the circle.
- Two students bounce the ball back and forth to each other.
- Student bounces the ball alone throughout the song.

PIANO/KEYBOARD INSTRUCTIONS
Students will use same hand position as in "Snail, Snail". Instruct the students that they will also play finger 3 in right hand. Students will touch the words located at the bottom of the page as they sing all of the song.

Play and Play: Teaching Kids to Play the Piano

10. LUCY LOCKET

Luc-y Loc-ket lost her poc-ket, Kit-ty Fish-er found it.
Not a pen-ny was there in it, on-ly rib-bon 'round it.

TEACHER INSTRUCTIONS
Sing the song and play the game before the students play the music on the piano/keyboard.

GAME DIRECTIONS
Object Needed
- small wallet with ribbon tied around it or picture of wallet with ribbon

Tell the story of Lucy Locket to introduce the game song.
One day Lucy Locket was walking to the bakery. She had her small wallet called a "pocket" with her. She passed many things on her way to the bakery and sometimes stopped to talked to friends. When she got to the bakery she realized that her pocket was missing. "Oh, no!," she said, "I have lost my pocket. I know I had it when I left the house. I must have dropped it along the way. I will walk back the same way and see if I can find it." Lucy Locket's friend, Kitty Fisher helped her find it. Our singing voices will be Kitty Fisher. When Lucy is walking and looking for her pocket and she is far away from it, we will sing with our soft voices. Lucy will know that the pocket is far away and will keep walking. When Lucy Locket is close to her pocket we will sing with our loud voices. Lucy will stop and look around whenever she hears our loud voices because she knows she is close to her pocket. Remember to use your pretty singing voice whenever you sing loudly. That is called "FORTE" in music. Our soft voice is called "PIANO", the same word as our piano musical instrument.
Choose a student to be Lucy Locket. Lucy hides his/her eye while you hide the wallet. Give the student a specific path to follow around the room as he/she looks for the wallet.

PIANO/KEYBOARD INSTRUCTIONS
Have students touch and sing the note names to the song. Have students put their fourth finger on F to play and sing the note names, then the words to the song. Guide students to play the piano loud and soft. Use the terms "Forte" and "Piano".
A challenge for students: "Play the song from memory. Play the song forte and piano as you watch Lucy Locket look for her pocket. Your loud and soft playing will help Lucy Locket find her pocket."

(page 22 *PLAY AND PLAY* Teacher Edition)

    a. Tell the story and then sing the song.
    b. Demonstrate how to play the game.
    c. Tell the students that all will get a turn to play the game at the next lesson.

11. Closing
    a. Students record attendance by putting stickers on charts.
    b. Students get a piece of candy.

DAY TWO

A. OBJECTIVES

The students will:
1. Develop a feeling of the steady beat.
2. Demonstrate an understanding of the black key groups by playing songs.
3. Develop an understanding of high and low sounds.
4. Develop an understanding of long and short sounds (quarter note and two eighth notes).

B. MATERIALS
1. Coin or small object such as a button
2. Tambourine or drum
3. Ball
4. Small wallet or picture of wallet
5. Frog picture

PROCEDURES
1. *HANDY, DANDY*

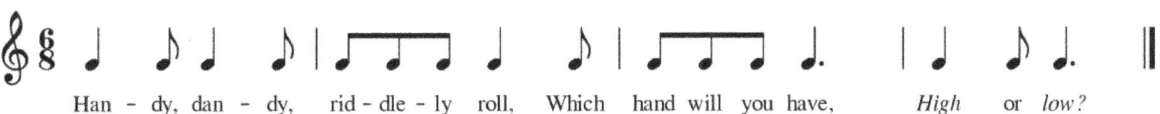

GAME DIRECTIONS
Object Needed
- Coin or other small object to hide in hand

Have a coin or other small object in one hand. Keep the *steady beat* by moving the object from one hand to the other on the steady beat as you say the poem, keeping the object hidden from the students. Put one closed hand high in the air on the word *"high"*, using a *high* sounding voice on that word. Put the other hand down low by your side on the word *"low"* while using a *low* sounding voice. Keep both hands closed. A student will guess which hand has the object. Say the poem again for each child.

a. Say the poem and play the game as instructed.
b. Face the same direction as the students as you say the poem again with right hand high and left hand low at the end of the poem.
c. Students name the right hand as high position and left hand as low position.
d. Give each student a penny to say the poem and do the motions, ending with right hand high and left hand low.

Transition: high and low finger numbers

2. *SNAIL, SNAIL,* page 36
    a. Students follow instructions on the song sheet and play the song on the piano/keyboard.

3. *IN AND OUT*, page 37
    a. Students will sing the song to review.
    b. Students will review finger numbers and black key groups.
    c. Students will review that finger numbers above the picture are played with right hand and finger numbers below the pictures are played with left hand.
    d. Students play the song on the piano/keyboard.
    e. Students play the game.
    f. Students follow instructions on the song sheet and play the song on the piano/keyboard.
    g. Students play the game.

4. *BOUNCE HIGH*, page 39
    a. Students follow instructions on the song sheet and play the song on the piano/keyboard.
    b. Students play the game.

5. BREAK

6. *APPLE, PEACH, PEAR, PLUM,* page 40

APPLE, PEACH, PEAR, PLUM

GAME DIRECTIONS
Objects Needed
- Hand drum or rhythm sticks

Tap the rhythm of the poem on the drum as the students say the poem.* Guide the students to develop an understanding that you tapped all of the sounds of the poem and that you tapped *"the way the words go."* Each student taps the rhythm and says the poem as the other students touch the pictures of the poem. Remind students to touch each picture *"the way the words go."* Students tell their birthday.

Touch each picture and say the words *"long"* and *"short-short"* to match the pictures under the heartbeats. The words *"long"* and *"short-short"* represent the rhythm sounds for each beat. Students will touch the pictures and say *"long"* and *"short-short"* in place of the words of the poem.

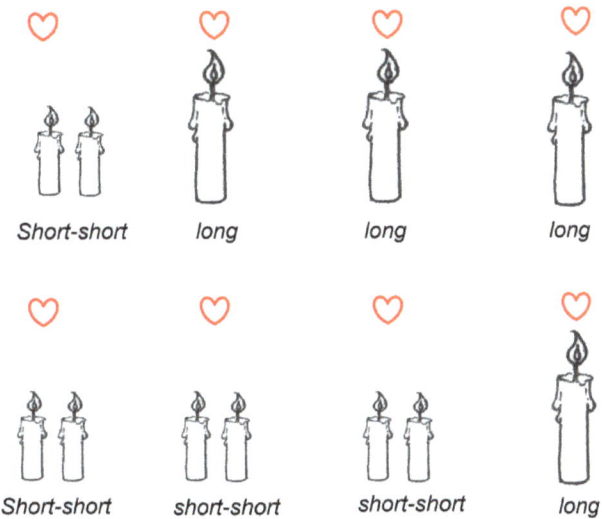

Guide the students to develop an understanding that there is one sound under the heartbeat for the *"long"* sound and there are two sounds under the heartbeat for the *"short-short"* sounds.

*The pictures under the heartbeats in this poem and upcoming poems and songs are sized to represent the rhythm. The one bigger picture under the heartbeat represents the quarter note in two beat or four beat meter. The two smaller pictures under one heartbeat represent two eighth notes in two beat or four beat meter.

(page 18 *PLAY AND PLAY* Teacher Edition)

a. Say the poem as you tap the steady beat on a rhythm instrument.
b. Students touch the heartbeats on the song sheet as they say the poem.
c. Follow the instructions above to introduce the rhythm, known as "long" and "short-short" sounds.
d. Students will follow instructions on their page as they read the long and short-short rhythm sounds.

7. *BOUNCE HIGH*, page 41
a. Lead students to discover this page has all of the song.
b. Students follow instructions on their songsheet.

Play and Play: Teaching Kids to Play the Piano

8. *LUCY LOCKET*, 42
a. Sing the song and play the game that was introduced on Day One.
b. Students follow instructions as found on their song sheet.

9. *FROG IN THE MEADOW*
a. Sing the song as the students listen then discuss.
b. Students play the game only today as instructed.

FROG IN THE MEADOW

TEACHER INSTRUCTIONS

Sing the song and play the game before students read and play the music on the piano/keyboard.

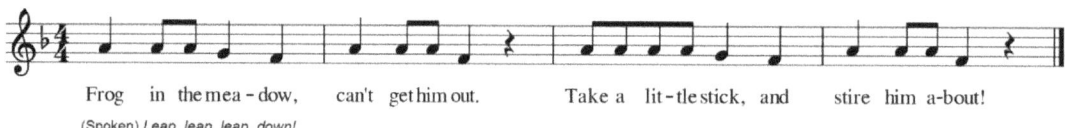

(Spoken) *Leap, leap, leap, down!*

GAME DIRECTIONS

Objects Needed
- small stick or mallet to use as "stirrer"

Leapfrog Version

Four students squat on the floor in a straight line. Once down on the floor, they "hide in the meadow" by putting knees and head on the floor, arms over their heads. The teacher taps the last child in line on the back with the stick on the words, *"take a little stick and stir him about"*. The last child stands, spreads legs, puts hands on back of each child in row in front of him as he leaps over them on the words, *"leap, leap, leap"*; then goes down to hide again in the front on the word, *"down."*

The Stirrer and the Frog Version

Students are scattered about the room, squatting on the floor. They "hide in the meadow" by putting knees and head on the floor, arms over their heads. One child is the "Stirrer" of the frogs. The student holds the stick and closes his/her eyes while the teacher chooses one of the frogs to be "It". The "Stirrer" opens eyes, walks among the frogs and sings, pretending to stir the frogs by moving stick in a circle in the air as he/she walks and sings. On the words, *"leap, leap, leap, down"*, all the frogs leap three times in any direction they choose, then hide back down. The student who is "It" immediately gets back up to leap and try to catch the "Stirrer". "Stirrer" is caught if the frog touches his foot or leg. Only the frog selected as "It" attempts to catch the "Stirrer." The frog can only chase the "Stirrer" by leaping.

PIANO/KEYBOARD INSTRUCTIONS

Have students touch the finger numbers on the page as they sing the finger numbers to the first phrase of the song. Guide the students to discover the music is played left to right and high and low. Tell the students: *"Start with the first finger number on the left side of the row and read left to right. Remember: You start high as you begin and then step down low."*

(page 32 PLAY AND PLAY Teacher Edition)

10. CLOSING: Attendance sticker and a piece of candy

DAY THREE

A. OBJECTIVES:

The students will:
1. Practice the steady beat.
2. Practice black key groups by playing songs on the keyboard.
3. Practice rhythm, the "long sound", quarter note, and "short-short sounds", eighth notes.
4. Practice high and low.

B. MATERIALS:
1. Coin or small object to hide in hands.
2. Ball
3. Small wallet
4. Frog picture attached to a stick.
5. Small key picture and poster board picture of flower garden.

C. PROCEDURES:
1. *HANDY, DANDY*
    a. Say the poem to review
    b. Students say the poem as they play the game.

Transition: "Let's play a song that uses the words high and low. Remember to look for the high and low finger numbers as you play."

2. *BOUNCE HIGH*, page 41
    a. Students play and sing the song.
    b. Students take turns playing the song on the keyboard as the other students bounce the ball and sing.
    c. Students play the song and sing the "long, short-short" rhythm names instead of the words.

Transition: Long and short-short patterns

3. *APPLE, PEACH, PEAR, PLUM,* page 40
    a. Students touch the pictures and say the words of the poem.
    b. Students touch the pictures and say the "short-short, long" rhythm words.
    c. Draw a short vertical line on the 2 short pictures and a long vertical line on the long picture of the student worksheet as shown:

This is the preparation before reading the music notation.

Play and Play: Teaching Kids to Play the Piano

   d. Tell the students that these lines are the symbols of the "short-short, long" sounds. Touch the lines and read the "short-short", long" pattern of the poem.
   e. Have the students draw the same lines on their worksheet then read the pattern.

Transition: Long and short-short sounds to another game song.

   4. LUCY LOCKET, page 42
      a. Sing the song and play the game.
      b. Students play and sing as instructed on their song sheet.

   5. BREAK - Snack time

   6. FROG IN THE MEADOW, page 43
      a. Sing the song to review.
      b. Sing and play the game.
      c. Students follow instructions on their song sheet as they play the song on their keyboard. Remind students that the empty line is a silent beat. They will just nod their head for the silent beat.

Transition: The frog was hiding in the green grass of the meadow. Here is a new song about something else that's hiding.

7. **CLOSET KEY**

TEACHER INSTRUCTIONS
Sing the song and play the game before students read and play the music on the piano/keyboard.

GAME DIRECTIONS
Objects Needed:
- Green old fashioned skeleton key made of sturdy material or a real key painted green.
- Flower garden picture or silk flowers and greenery pasted to poster board.

Tell the story to introduce the game song.
One day someone just your age was walking to town with Mother. Mother stopped suddenly, turned to her child and said, "Oh dear! I forgot to lock the closet. There is something very important in it! I am going to give you the key. You are old enough to walk home by yourself and lock the closet. Then come straight back and meet me at the bakery." The child took the key and started back home. On the way, he had to pass a beautiful flower garden in the neighbor lady's front yard. He stopped to look and accidentally dropped the closet key! It was hard to find because the key was green, just like the grass and stems and leaves of the flowers. The lady saw him drop the key and said, "I will help. You stand here at the garden gate and just look all around for it. Do not walk in the garden. You can point when you see the key and I will get it for you."

One student hides his/her eyes while the teacher or another student "hides" the green key in the flower garden with just a small part of the key showing. The teacher and the other students sing the song as the student stands behind a child representing the garden gate and looks for the key. The teacher is the "lady/gentleman of the garden." Once the student spots the key, the teacher picks up the key. The game continues as each student has a turn to look for the key.

PIANO/KEYBOARD INSTRUCTIONS
This song introduces the meter signature, bar lines, measure and double bar line.

Identify $\genfrac{}{}{0pt}{}{2}{\heartsuit}$ as the symbol that tells that the heartbeats are in groups of 2. Identify the bar lines as the lines that separate the heartbeats into groups of 2. Identify the measures as the area between the bar lines where the notes are written. Identify the double bar line as the symbol placed at the end of the song.

Guide the students to touch the heartbeats and identify 2 beats in each measure.

Guide the students to identify the skip from finger 2 to finger 4. Remind students that they will skip a black key as they skip finger 3. Guide the students to identify the steps with fingers 4-3-2 in the last measure.

(page 30 *PLAY AND PLAY* Teacher Edition)

    a. Tell the story as found in the instructions.
    b. Sing the song as the students listen, discuss, and play the game only this day as shown in the Teacher Instructions.

8. CLOSING-sticker and piece of candy for attendance

Play and Play: Teaching Kids to Play the Piano

DAY FOUR

A. OBJECTIVES:
   THE STUDENTS WILL:
   1. Develop an understanding of rhythm symbols to represent the sounds on the beat: quarter note, eighth notes, and quarter rest.
   2. Demonstrate an understanding of rhythms by playing known songs with rhythm symbols.
   3. Practice the steady beat.

B. MATERIALS:
   1. Stick with the frog picture attached.
   2. Drum
   3. Key and flower garden picture
   4. Drum, tambourine, or rhythm sticks
   5. Rhythm Flashcards with quarter note and eighth notes.

C. PROCEDURES:
   1. *FROG IN THE MEADOW*, page 43
      a. Play and sing the song on the keyboards.
      b. Play and sing the "long, short-short" rhythm sounds.

   2. *APPLE, PEACH, PEAR, PLUM,* pages 40 and 44
      a. Students will touch the pictures and read the poem.
      b. Read the "long, short-short" rhythm names as they play rhythm instruments.
      c. Tell the students that the lines they drew for the
      d. "short-short, long" sounds are shortcuts for drawing music notes and that now you will add noteheads to make the music symbol.
      e. Draw noteheads and shade them in to represent the 2 eighth notes and the quarter note. Draw a beam across the top to connect the eighth notes, as shown:

    f. Name the "long" sound as quarter note and the "short-short" sounds as eighth notes. Tell the students we will use the shortcut rhythm names of ta (pronounced "tah") for the quarter note and ti-ti (pronounced "tee-tee") for the eighth notes.

    g. Have the students draw and shade in the noteheads and add the beams to the eighth notes on their song sheet from the previous day.

    h. Students read the rhythm of page 46. Instruct the students that the notes of the ti-ti's and ta's are the same height.

3. BREAK - snack time
4. *CLOSET KEY,* page 45 and 46
  a. Sing the song and play the game.
  b. Have the students draw the "short-short, long" vertical lines as they did on the song, *APPLE, PEACH, PEAR, PLUM.*
  c. Follow instructions as given on the student page.
  d. Students will get the song sheet that has just the rhythm and follow the instructions as given.

Transition: reading 4 beat rhythm patterns of known songs

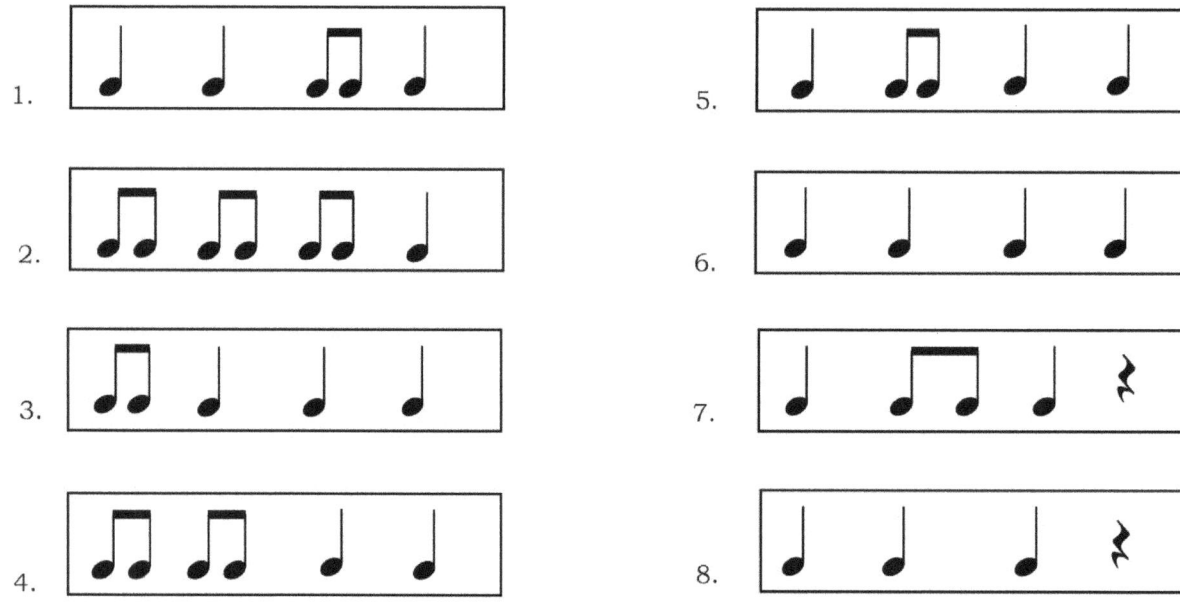

5. FOUR BEAT RHYTHM FLASHCARDS
   a. Students will read and clap the rhythm one card at a time as you hold up the cards that you have made. (Cards 1-6 are for this lesson. Cards 7-8 which have the quarter rest symbol ↯ will be added at the next lesson.)
   b. Students will read and play the rhythm on a rhythm instrument.
   c. Challenge: Hold up a card for the students to read silently, then place the card face down so that the students play and say the rhythm pattern from memory.

6. CLOSING- Sticker and piece of candy for attendance

DAY FIVE
A. OBJECTIVES:
   THE STUDENTS WILL:
   1. Develop an understanding that the quarter rest symbol ↯ represents one silent beat.

2. Practice rhythms and the steady beat by playing game songs.

3. Practice known rhythms by reading 4 beat rhythm flashcards.

4. Demonstrate music reading skills by playing game songs on the keyboard/piano.

B. MATERIALS:
1. Rhythm flashcards with quarter note, eighth notes, quarter rest.
2. Rhythm instruments.
3. Materials for game songs used during the week.

C. PROCEDURES
1. FROG IN THE MEADOW, pages 43 and 47
    a. Play the keyboards and sing the rhythm names.
    b. Play and sing the words.
    c. Play the game.
    d. Students will get the song sheet with the music symbols.
    e. Draw the quarter rest symbol on the board, name it as rest, and define it as the symbol for one silent beat.
    f. Students will find and circle the rests on their song sheet then follow the instructions as given on their song sheet.
    g. Guide the students to understand that the notes have stems pointing down to indicate they will play with their left hand.

Transition: Students will play two game songs with music symbols that use a ball.

2. *BOUNCE HIGH, page 48* Students will follow instructions on their song sheet.

3. *PLAINSIES, CLAPSIES, page 49*

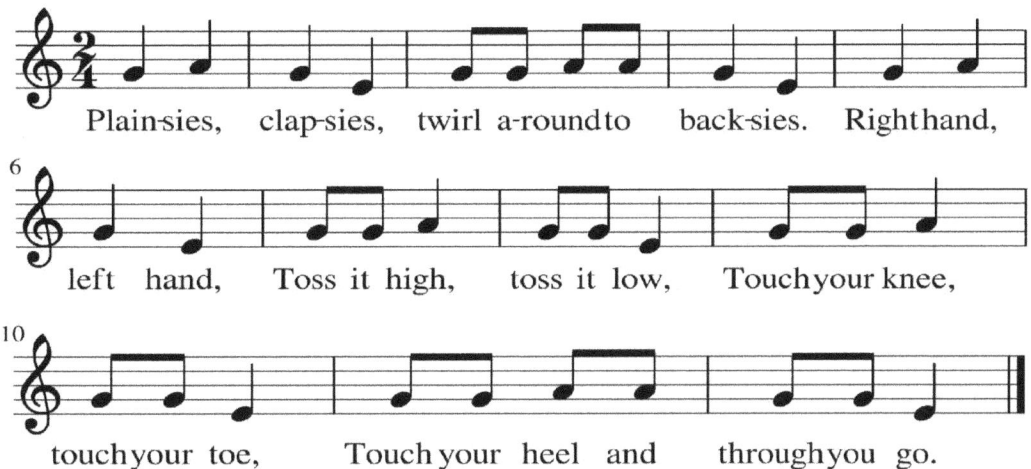

Play and Play: Teaching Kids to Play the Piano

TEACHER INSTRUCTIONS

Sing the song and play the game before the students play the music on the piano/keyboard.

GAME DIRECTIONS
Object Needed
•Ball

The ball is not bounced but tossed, along with other hand motions listed below.

SONG WORDS	HAND MOTIONS
"Plainsies,	Toss ball up and catch it.
clapsies,	Toss ball up, clap hands, catch it.
Twirl around to backsies	Pass ball around back from one hand to other *Alternate motions:* Toss ball up, twirl hands around back while ball is in the air.
Right hand,	Hold ball out to side with right hand.
left hand,	Hold ball out to side with left hand.
Toss it high,	Toss ball high in air and catch it.
toss it low	Toss ball low in air and catch it.
Touch your knee, touch your toe, touch your heel	Toss the ball up, touch knee, catch ball; repeat toss and catch while touching toe then heel.
And through you go."	Move ball between legs in a figure eight motion.

PIANO/KEYBOARD INSTRUCTIONS

Guide students to discover that the first two lines of the song are the same as the previous song, BOUNCE HIGH, and they will use the same finger position.

Have students take turns playing and singing the song on the piano/keyboard while others play the game.

(page 54 PLAY AND PLAY teacher edition)

4. BREAK
5. RHYTHM FLASHCARDS
    a. Use the flashcards from the previous lesson, including cards 7 and 8 with the quarter rest.
    b. Students read and clap all the cards.
    c. Students read and clap the cards with a continuous steady beat as you hold them up.

Transition: Rhythm cards 2 and 4

6. *LUCY LOCKET*, page 50
    a. Students read and clap both cards.
    b. Change the last note in card 2 to become 2 eighth notes. The students will read and clap the new pattern, "ti-ti, ti-ti, ti-ti, ti-ti." Then have them read and clap this new pattern followed by card 4.
    c. Students just clap and read the rhythm inside their heads.
    d. Hum LUCY LOCKET as they just clap again. Students name the song.
    e. Students read and clap the rhythm from their song sheet.
    f. Students will play and sing the song and play the game.

7. DEMONSTRATION FOR PARENTS
    a. Invite parents in for the last 30 minutes of the lesson as students demonstrate what they've learned.
    b. Explain to the parents the process the students have gone through to become music readers this week, going from pictures to represent the rhythm to the music symbols.
    c. My song demonstration order:
        i. Handy Dandy, page 15
        ii. Apple, Peach, Pear, Plum, rhythm pictures, page 40
        iii. Apple, Peach, Pear, Plum, rhythm notation, page 44
        iv. Frog in the Meadow, page 47
        v. Plainsies, Clapsies, page 49
        vi. Lucy Locket, page 50
    d. Serve refreshments and students get an attendance sticker, piece of candy, and choose a prize from the treasure box.

This demonstration for parents is a good time to discuss scheduling their child for lessons in the upcoming piano year. Let parents know they will be getting an email from you soon with all the details.

CURRENT/RETURNING STUDENTS PIANO SUMMER CAMP

Summer Piano Camp for current students of the piano studio is a good way to retain students and it gives them an opportunity to continue their piano study over the summer.

1. Let parents know about the camp in your studio's monthly newsletter, beginning in April.

2. Group the students according to age and ability.

3. Plan the camp around a theme. Here are some that I have used:
    a. CHRISTMAS IN JULY. Students learned Christmas carols and had hot chocolate, snow cones, etc. for snacks.
    b. PATRIOTIC THEME. Students learned patriotic songs and marches and had a 4th of July theme picnic. Snacks each day followed the theme such as ice cream, coke floats, and popcorn.
    c. GRAND PIANO AND CONCERT HALL. We took a field trip on the last day of camp to the local university. Students explored the mechanical workings of the grand piano, led by a piano professor of the university. Students played a piece on the grand piano and the professor played for them.
    d. MUSIC AND ART. Students worked on music from a particular era and took a field trip to a museum that had an exhibit of paintings of that era.
    e. FINE ARTS CAMP. This was a 3 hour camp and I charged double the summer camp tuition for this extended camp. The sessions of the camp included:
        - Piano session.
        - Drawing session taught by an art teacher.
        - Movement session. We did Maypole dances.
        - Field trip to the Museum of Fine Arts in Houston, Texas to see the Choreographic Objects interactive exhibit.

Just like the beginners camp, be sure on the last camp day to let parents know they will be getting an email from you soon about the upcoming piano year.

OPERATING A PROFITABLE YEAR ROUND PIANO STUDIO

Now that you have conducted a successful piano camp, and you have recruited students, it's time to set up your piano studio for success. I am going to share with you my steps and procedures.

I teach students in a small group setting. My groups are:
- Young beginners, 5-10 year olds.
- Older beginning students, usually 11 years old and older
- Returning students.

All students, including returning students, are grouped by age and ability, usually 3 or 4 students per group.

A 61 key keyboard is provided for every student in the class. The piano is also used.

BENEFITS OF GROUP PIANO LESSONS

TEACHER BENEFITS
- Teaching hours are consolidated.
- Teachers generate more income in less teaching time.

STUDENT BENEFITS
- Children learn in a fun setting with music they can relate to and enjoy playing.
- Singing games make the children want to play the piano.
- Children learn from both the teacher and other students in piano class.
- Reinforces the benefits of music lessons in other areas:
  - Academic skills, in particular Language Arts, Mathematics and Social Studies.
  - Physical skills.
  - Social skills.

PARENT BENEFITS
- Children are motivated to attend weekly lessons in the piano class setting.
- Group lesson format means a longer class time for children and a longer break for parents.

YOUNG BEGINNERS GROUP LESSONS

Young beginners use the piano book, **PLAY AND PLAY**. This book uses a unique approach to teaching beginning piano for young students. Students play singing games then learn to read the music to these singing games on the piano and/or keyboard. In addition, each page is a color sheet. Students color the pictures as the teacher works one-on-one with each student. Please see my website, www.dianeenglepianostudio.com for more information about both the student and teacher editions of **PLAY AND PLAY**.

OLDER STUDENTS GROUP LESSONS

The benefit of group lessons for older students is the opportunity for social interaction. Students this age are very social and enjoy interacting with their peers. I have found they prefer this format over the one-on-one 30 minute lesson with the teacher. Students also enjoy the healthy competition of perfecting a piece of music as well as scales and chords. They also enjoy the challenge of playing games and doing activities that use both rhythmic and melodic concepts.

There are several good graded piano series that can be adapted to group lessons.

THE PIANO YEAR

I follow the same steps that are used for the summer camp whenever I contact parents about the upcoming piano year, which for my studio is September through May.

- Notices are sent to parents through the piano studio's monthly newsletter.
- Advertise on social media and in the local newspaper.
- Enrollment form sent to parents.
- Email parents during the summer giving detailed information about their child's weekly piano schedule, the tuition cost, studio policy and procedures, etc.
- Mail letter to students one week prior to the first lesson.
- Email reminder to parents one week prior to the first lesson.
- Text reminder to parents the day before the first lesson.

THE SCHEDULE

The piano classes are scheduled once a week, 45 minutes per class. My classes follow the regular school day, with the first group lesson of the day beginning at 4:15 p.m. I have 4 groups per day. My classes are scheduled three days per week, Tuesday - Thursday.

Many parents that homeschool their children can be flexible on the time schedule. Perhaps you can schedule some classes earlier in the day.

STUDIO POLICIES

Your piano studio is a viable business. You are a professional educator and a business person. Parents and students will see you and your business this way if you present yourself and your studio to them in this manner.

TUITION

Let's start with tuition payment policies. Tuition payments are paid monthly, due in full at the first lesson of the month. I do not deduct for missed lessons. Instead, make-up lessons are offered for any absence. This avoids the question about deducting for missed lessons.

If a student is 10 minutes late, I text the parent to ask, "Is 'Johnny' on the way to piano or do we need to schedule a make-up lesson?" That particular lesson of the month is accounted for immediately and the make-up lesson is scheduled if needed.

I charge the full tuition price for every student, even if they are part of the same family.

I use a spreadsheet for all the studio's financial transactions. If tuition is not received at the first lesson, an invoice is sent out.

NEWSLETTER

I email a monthly newsletter to parents. I often send it as a text. I list the schedule for the upcoming month along with other news of the studio. Pictures are included.

ADVERTISING

Today's technology makes it easy to advertise your piano studio.
- **WEBSITE.** An up-to-date website is a must in today's technology. Pictures are a very important part of my regular posts along with a weekly blog post.
- **SOCIAL MEDIA.** Regular posts of pictures and short posts of the happenings of the studio on social media are other ways to keep your piano studio out front of the public.

RECITAL

My piano recital is scheduled in May at the end of the piano year. My philosophy about a piano recital is that it should be a pleasurable experience for the students, not something they are overly worried about. I choose an individual piece for each student that is challenging but not overwhelming. The recital piece should reflect the student's progress over the piano year.

Students also play one ensemble piece, in particular one of the game songs of the year. They *play and play*, just like the title of their book and just like they do in their piano class. Students play the song on the keyboards then play the game for the audience. Older students take over playing the song at the keyboards as the younger students play the game. The older students' version of the song is more sophisticated, using chords or an accompaniment version of the song.

I have found that the audience enjoys the game song part of the recital. It helps to make the recital a more relaxing and fun time for the students. Plus, it is quite entertaining for the audience!

The program for the recital is diverse. I start with two of my most advanced students playing a duet. Next come a few students in the middle range of music reading ability. Then, a small group of the young beginners play a game song at the keyboards and then play the game. The middle range of students who played before the game will play the song as the students play the game. After the game, these same young beginners take their turn at playing their solo piece. I continue in this program format throughout the recital. I find that the younger students are inspired as they listen to the more advanced students and they are willing and ready to play themselves.

I usually have 3 game songs scattered throughout the recital. My two of the most advanced students play after the third game to end the recital.

There is a reception to follow the recital. Refreshments are simple, such as cake and small bottles of water.

The reception can be an inexpensive yet very positive way to end the piano year and to keep your piano studio in parents' and friends' minds for the upcoming year.

FIND OUT MORE
You can get more information and ideas for your piano studio by visiting my website, www.dianeenglepianostudio.com and by following me on my Facebook page, **Diane's Piano Studio** as well as on Instagram, **#dianespiano.**

I wish you lots of success in your piano studio. Remember, I'm in a small town. I have a profitable piano studio and so can you!

Students are playing the game song, "CLOSET KEY" outside.

SONG SHEETS APPENDIX

PIANO KEYBOARD

INSTRUCTIONS
Circle the two black key group.
Find a group of two black keys on the keyboard with your left hand. Use fingers 2 and 3 to play the black keys in the two black key group.
Find a group of two black keys on the keyboard with your right hand. Use fingers 2 and 3 to play the black keys in the two black key group.

Circle the three black key group.
Find a group of three black keys on the keyboard with your left hand. Use fingers 2, 3, and 4 to play the black keys in the three black key group.
Find a group of three black keys on the keyboard with your right hand. Use fingers 2, 3, and 4 to play the black keys in the three black key group.

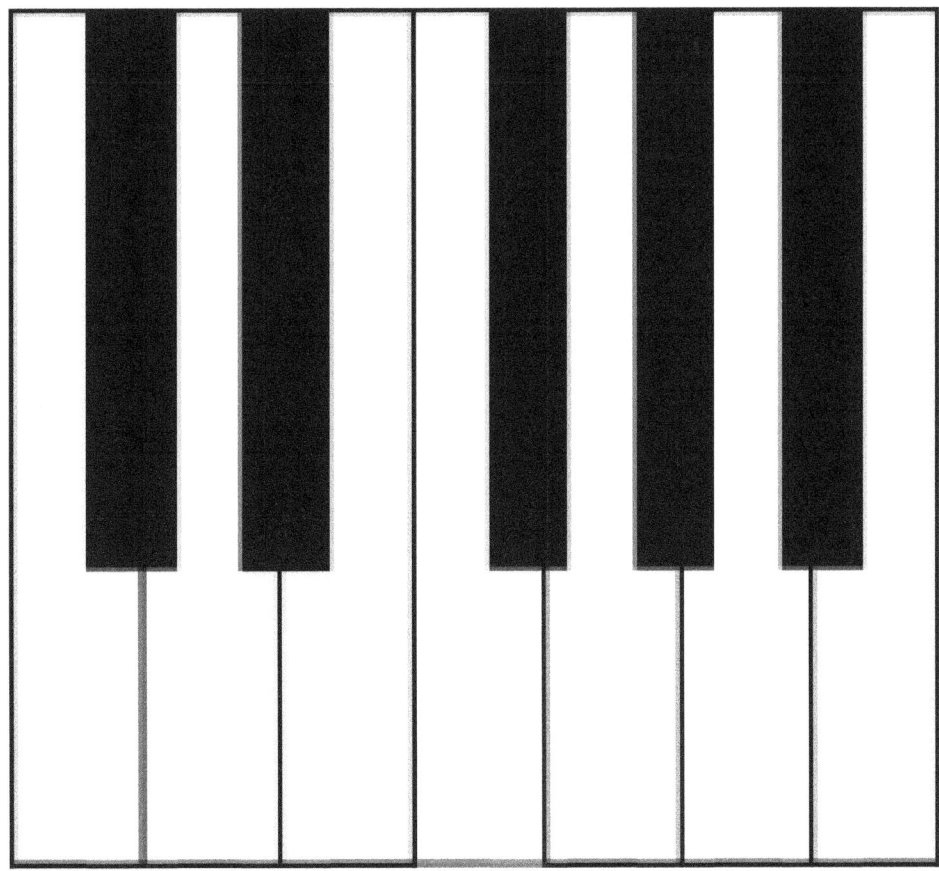

SNAIL, SNAIL

INSTRUCTIONS
Put your right hand finger 2 on the group of three black keys.
Put your left hand finger 2 on the group of two black keys.
Play and sing the finger numbers.
Play and sing the words. Your teacher will help you sing the words under the under the snail picture.

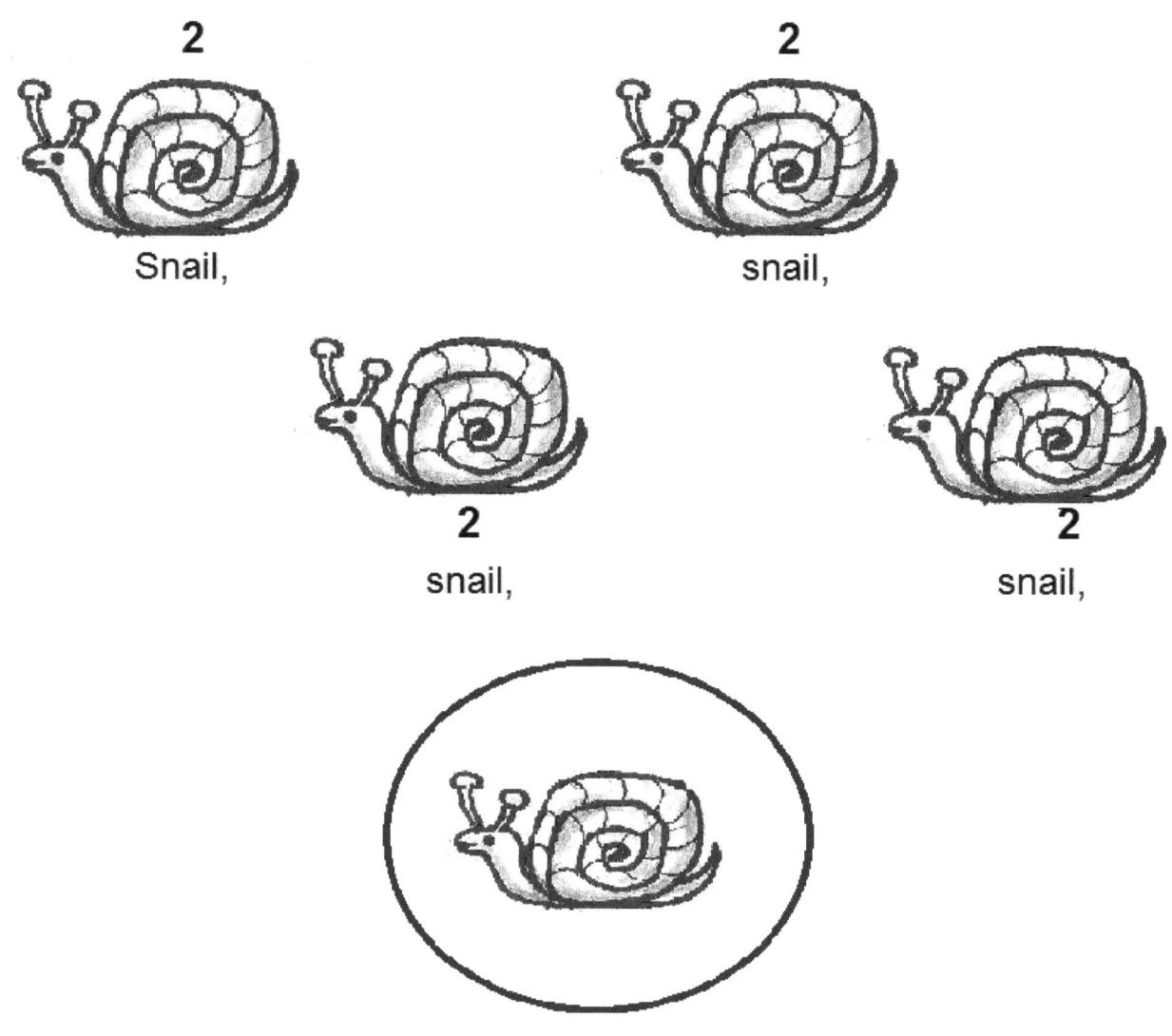

Go around, and 'round and 'round.

Resource Guide

IN AND OUT

INSTRUCTIONS
Put your right hand finger 2 on the group of **three** black keys. Put your left hand finger 2 on the group of two black keys. Play with your right hand when finger 2 is above the bean bag. Play with your left hand when finger 2 is below the bean bag.
The heartbeat with no picture means a silent heartbeat. Do not play. Just nod your head on the silent heartbeat.
Play and sing the words.
Color the bean bags.

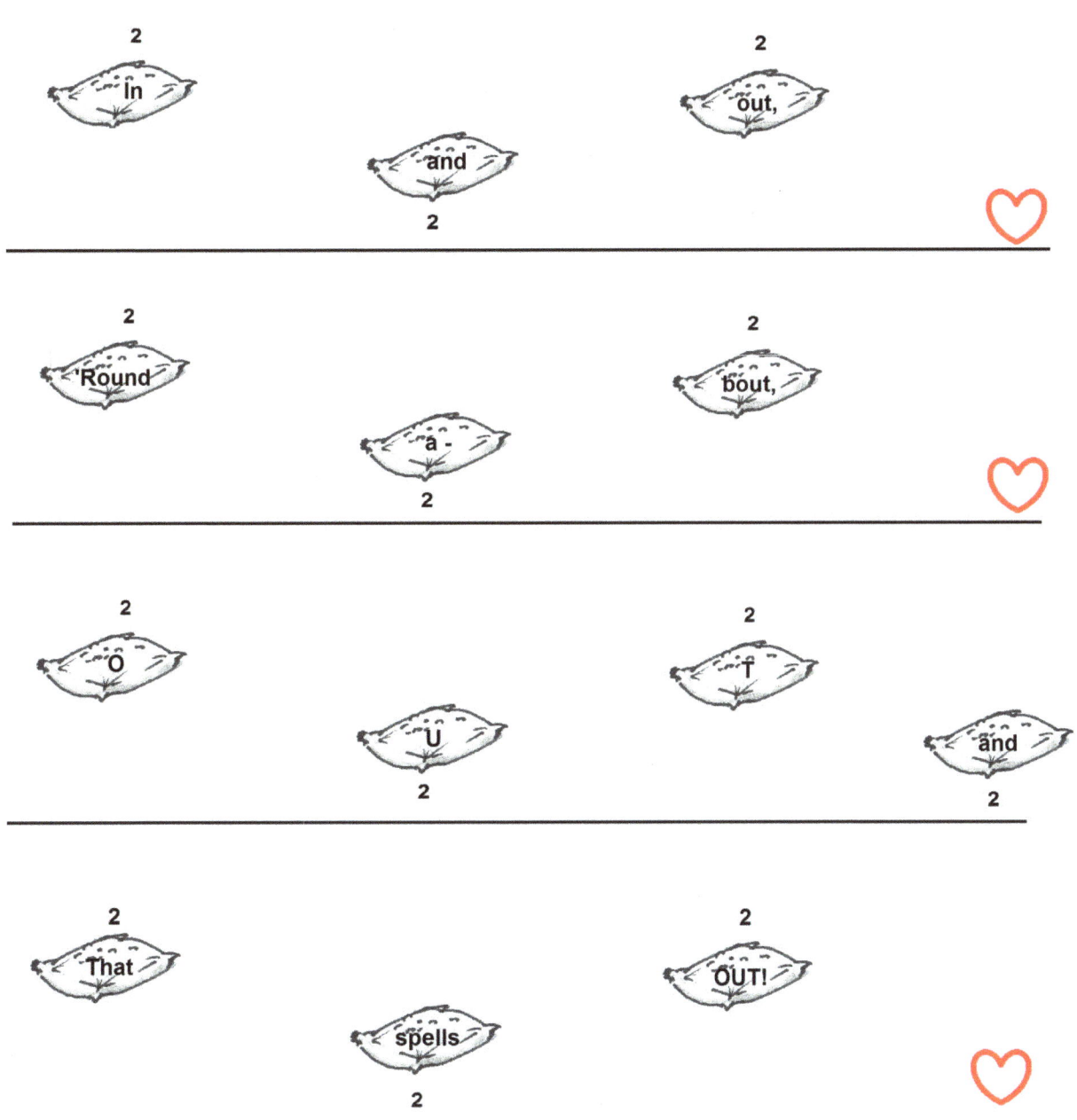

HEARTBEAT CHART

INSTRUCTIONS
Touch each heartbeat as your teacher plays the drum.
Touch each heartbeat as you say the poem.

BOUNCE HIGH

INSTRUCTIONS
Put your right hand on a group of three black keys.
Put your left hand on a group of two black keys.
Play and sing the finger numbers.
Remember to play with your right hand when the finger numbers are above the picture and with your left hand when the finger numbers are below the picture.
Play and sing the words.

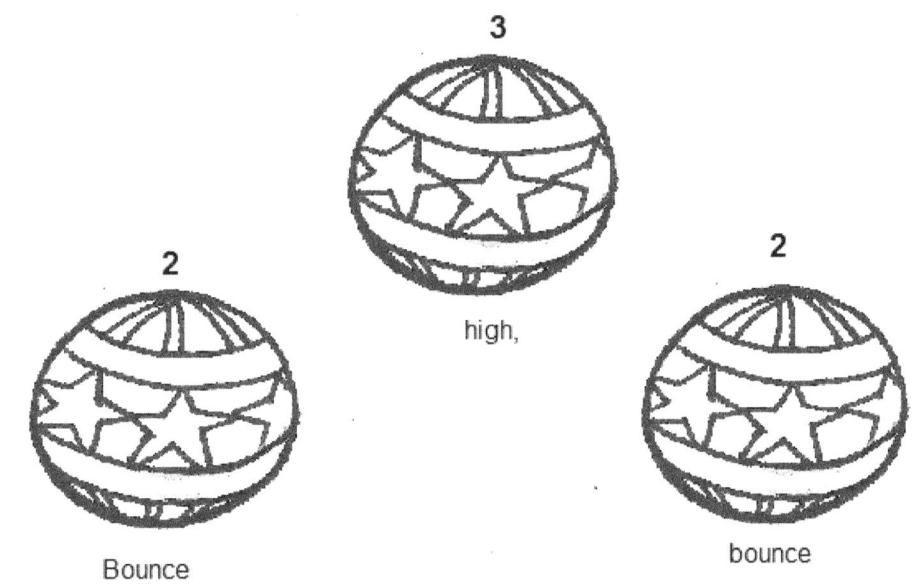

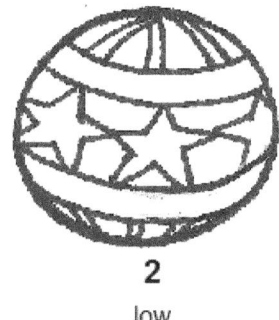

Bounce the ball to Shiloh.

APPLE, PEACH, PEAR, PLUM

INSTRUCTIONS
Say the poem and clap the way the words go.
Touch the pictures and say the poem. Be sure to touch each picture.
Touch the pictures and say the long and short-short sounds.
Clap and say the long and short-short sounds.

Ap · ple,   peach,   pear,   plum;

Tell me   when your   birth- day   comes.

BOUNCE HIGH

INSTRUCTIONS
Touch the pictures and say the long and short-short sounds.
Clap and read the long and short-short sounds.
Put your right hand on the group of three black keys.
Put your left hand on the group of two black keys.
Play and sing the long and short-short sounds then play and sing the words.

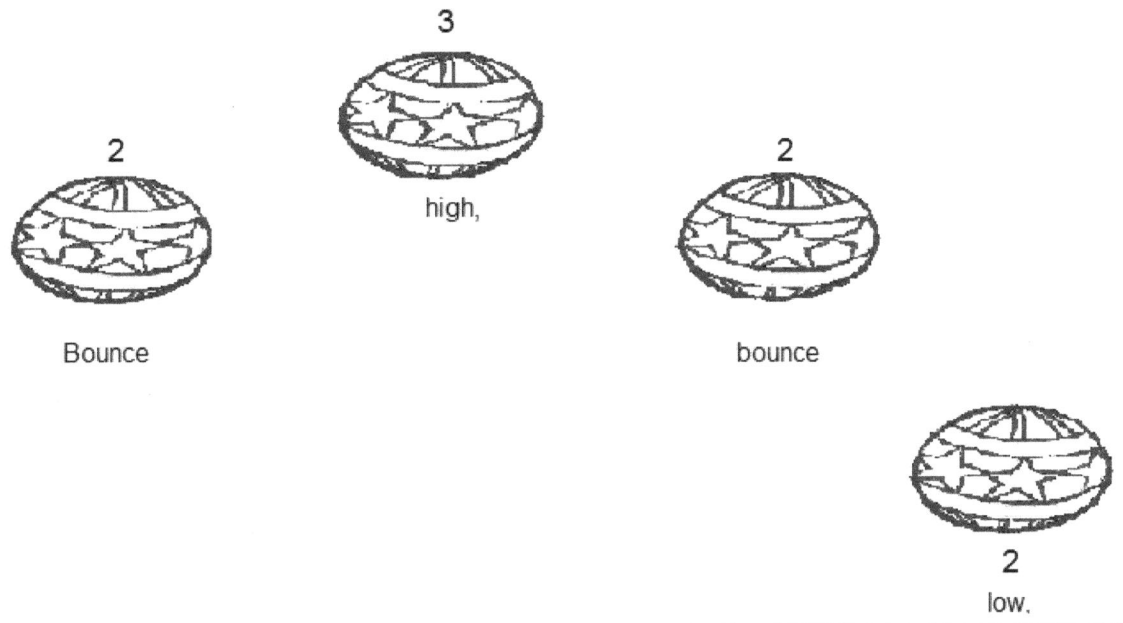

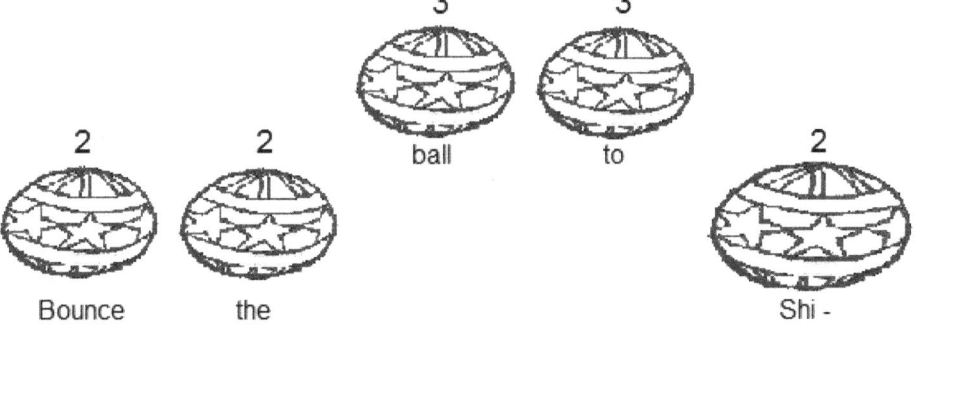

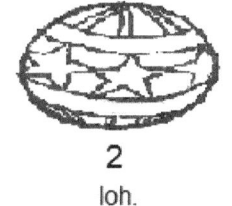

Play and Play: Teaching Kids to Play the Piano

LUCY LOCKET

INSTRUCTIONS
Put your right hand on the group of three black keys.
Put your left hand on the group of two black keys.
Play and sing the finger numbers.
Play and sing the long and short-short sounds then play and sing the words.

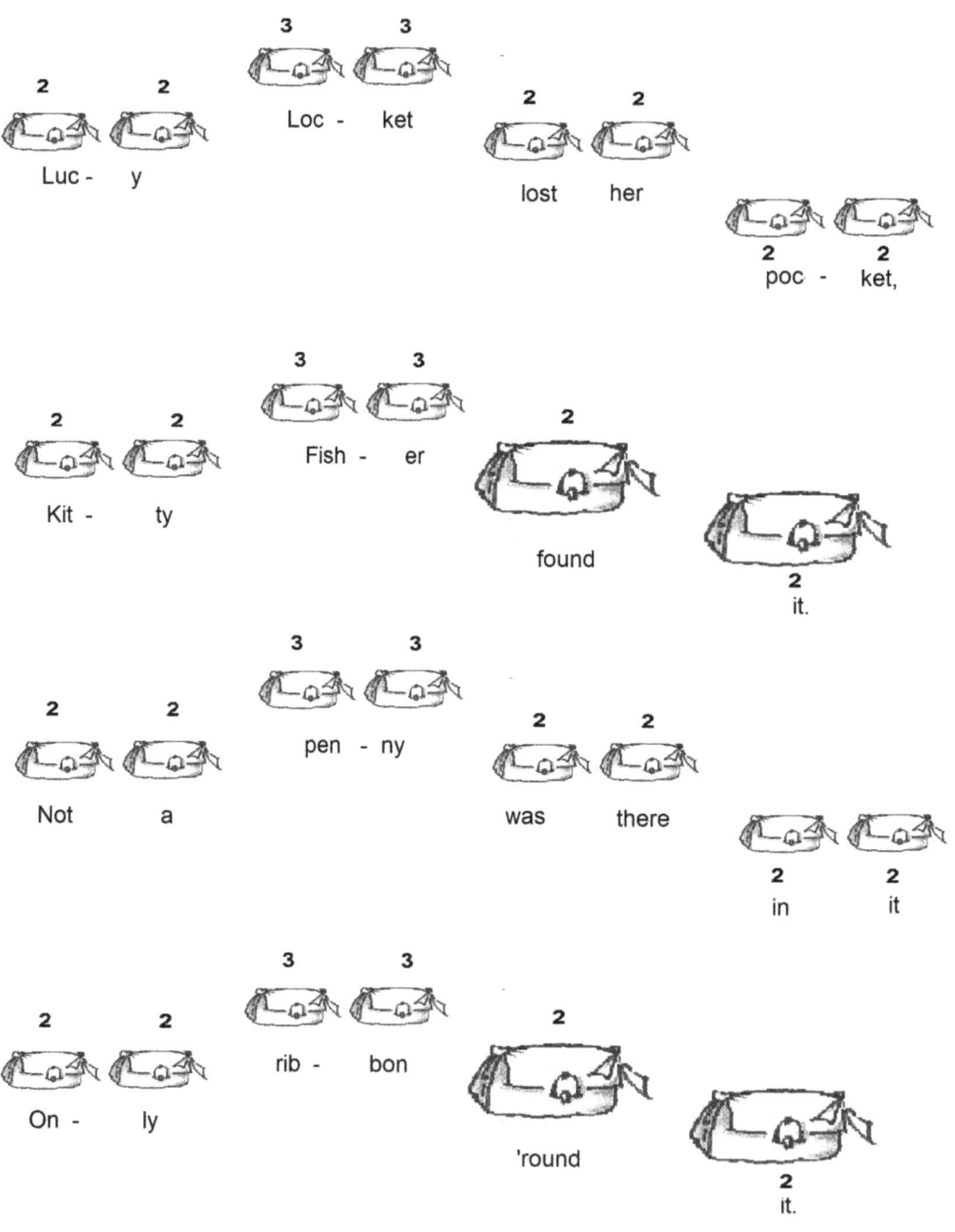

FROG IN THE MEADOW

INSTRUCTIONS
Touch the heartbeats and read the rhythm.
Put your left hand on the group of 3 black keys.
Play and sing the finger numbers.
Play and sing the rhythm names then play and sing the words.

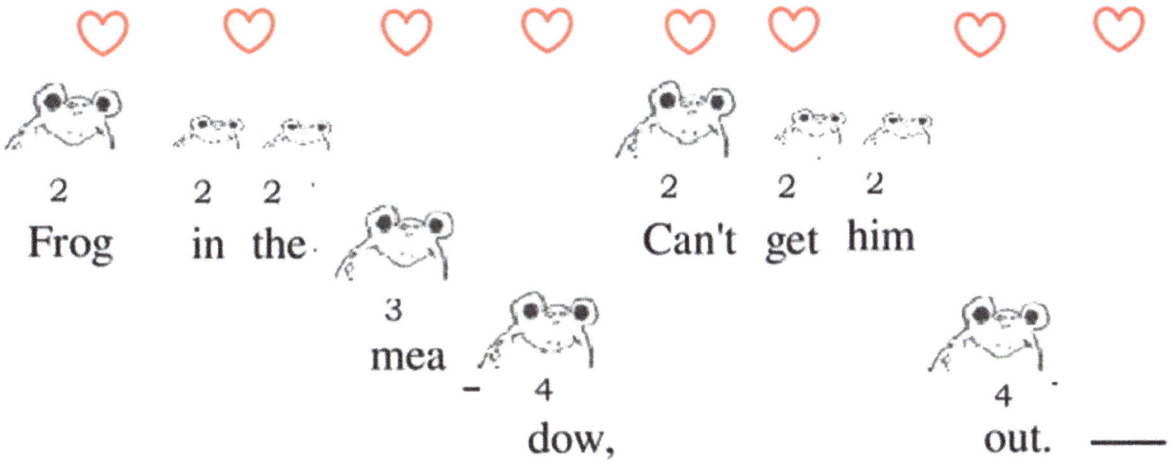

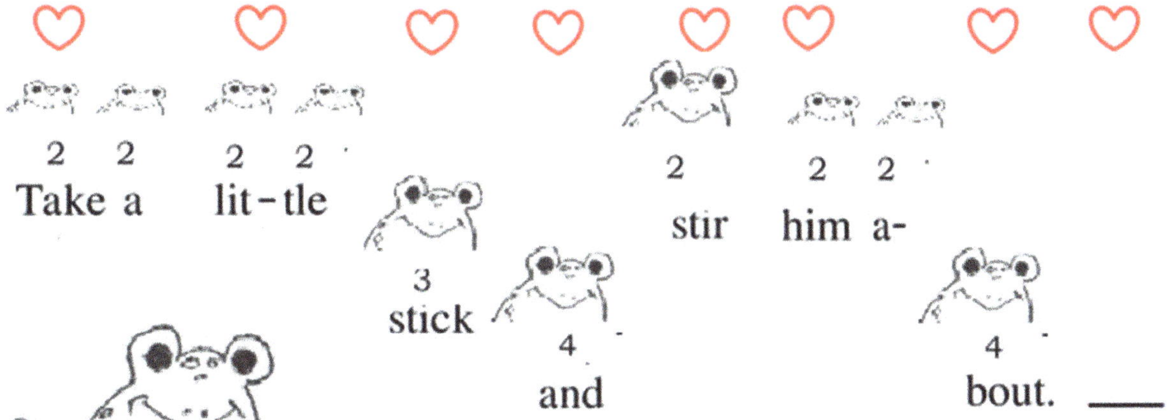

♡ ♡ ♡ ♡ ♡ ♡ ♡ ♡

2   2 2   2   2 2
Frog in the   Can't get him
        3
        mea
         - 4   4
          dow,   out. —

♡ ♡ ♡ ♡ ♡ ♡ ♡ ♡

2 2   2 2   2   2 2
Take a lit-tle   stir him a-
        3
        stick
         4   4
         and   bout. —

Play and Play: Teaching Kids to Play the Piano   43

APPLE, PEACH, PEAR, PLUM

INSTRUCTIONS
Touch each heartbeat as you say the poem.
Touch each word or part of the word as you say the poem.
Clap the rhythm as you say the poem. Remember, the rhythm is "*the way the words go.*"
Clap and read the rhythm names.

Ap - ple, peach, pear, plum;

Tell me when your birth - day comes.

44 Resource Guide

CLOSET KEY

INSTRUCTIONS
Touch the heartbeats and read the rhythm.
Touch the notes and read the rhythm.
Clap and read the rhythm.
Put your right hand on the group of 3 black keys.
Play and sing the finger numbers.
Play and sing the rhythm names then play and sing the words.

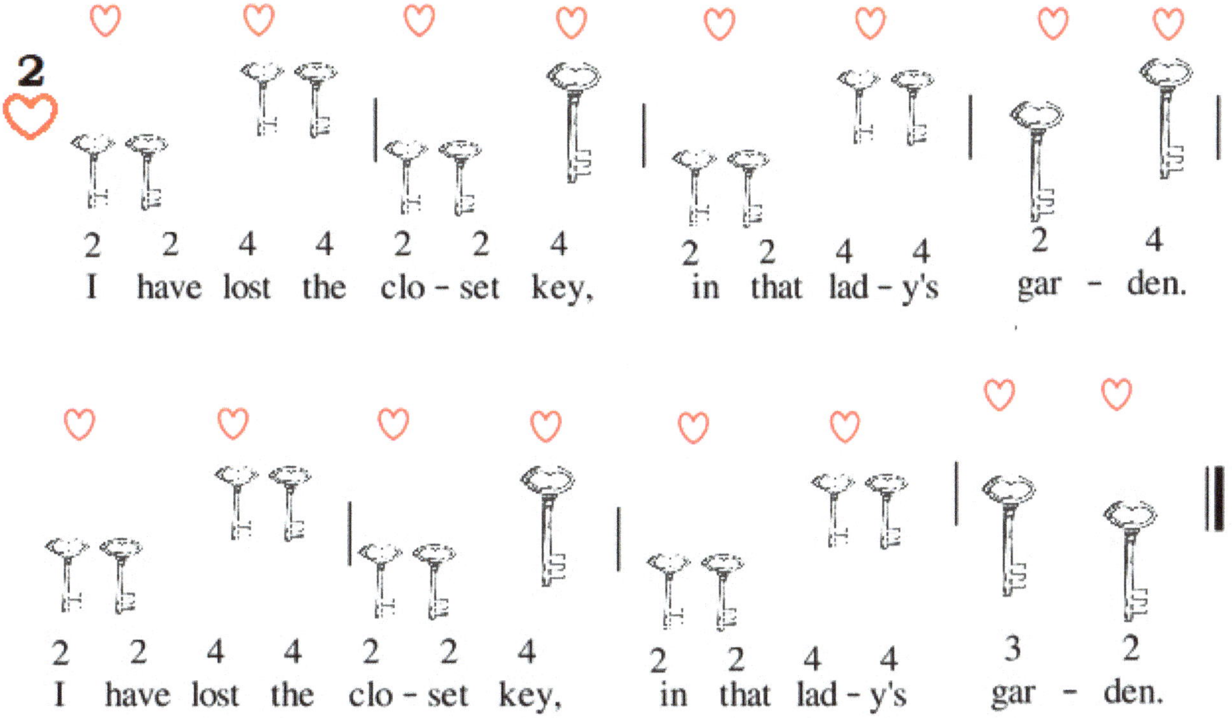

2	2	4	4	2	2	4	2	2	4	4	2	4
I	have	lost	the	clo-	set	key,	in	that	lad-	y's	gar-	den.

2	2	4	4	2	2	4	2	2	4	4	3	2
I	have	lost	the	clo-	set	key,	in	that	lad-	y's	gar-	den.

Play and Play: Teaching Kids to Play the Piano

CLOSET KEY

INSTRUCTIONS
Touch the heartbeats and read the rhythm.
Touch the notes and read the rhythm.
Clap and read the rhythm.
Put your right hand on the group of three black keys.
Play and sing the finger numbers.
Play and sing the rhythm names then play and sing the words.

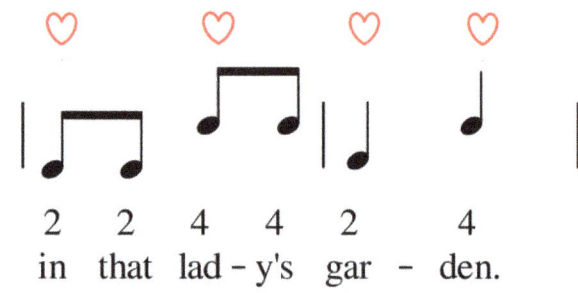

2 2 4 4 2 2 4   2 2 4 4 2 4
I have lost the clo-set key,   in that lad-y's gar - den.

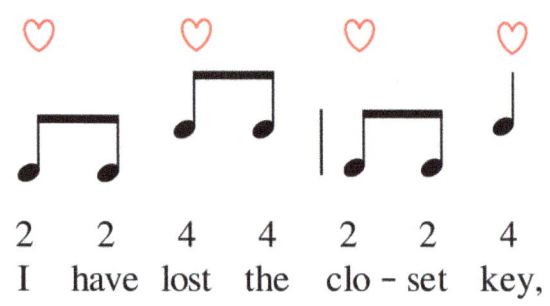
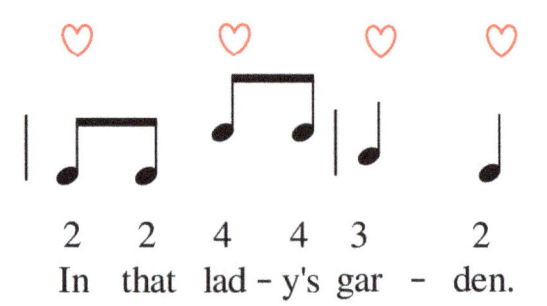

2 2 4 4 2 2 4   2 2 4 4 3 2
I have lost the clo-set key,   In that lad-y's gar - den.

Resource Guide

FROG IN THE MEADOW

INSTRUCTIONS
Touch the heartbeats and read the rhythm.
Touch the notes and read the rhythm.
Clap and read the rhythm.
Put your left hand on the group of 3 black keys.
Play and sing the finger numbers.
Play and sing the rhythm names then play and sing the words.

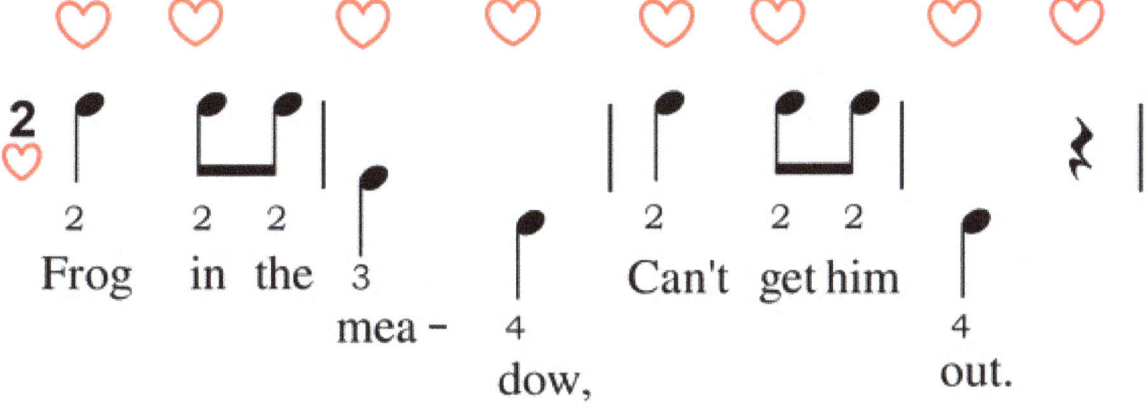

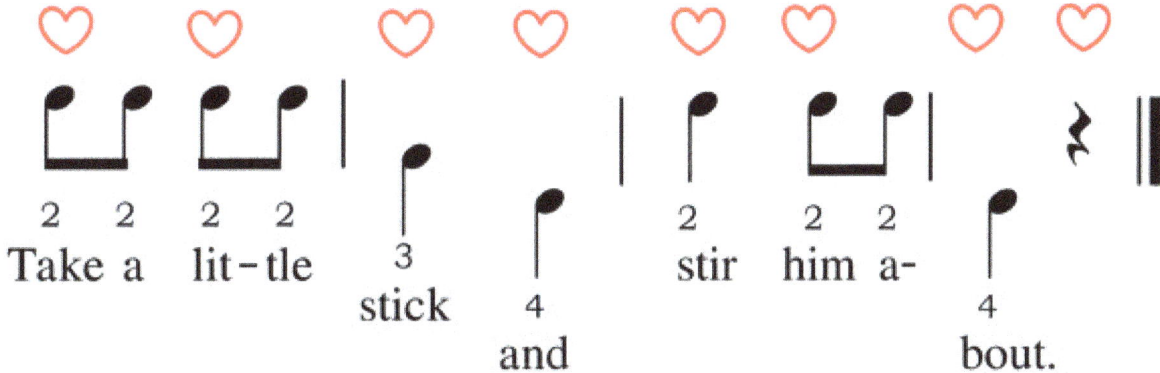

BOUNCE HIGH

INSTRUCTIONS
Pat the heartbeat and read the rhythm.
Touch the notes and read the rhythm.
Clap and read the rhythm.
Put your right hand on the group of three black keys. Your left hand will be on the group of two black keys.
Play and sing the finger numbers.
Play and sing the rhythm names then play and sing the words.

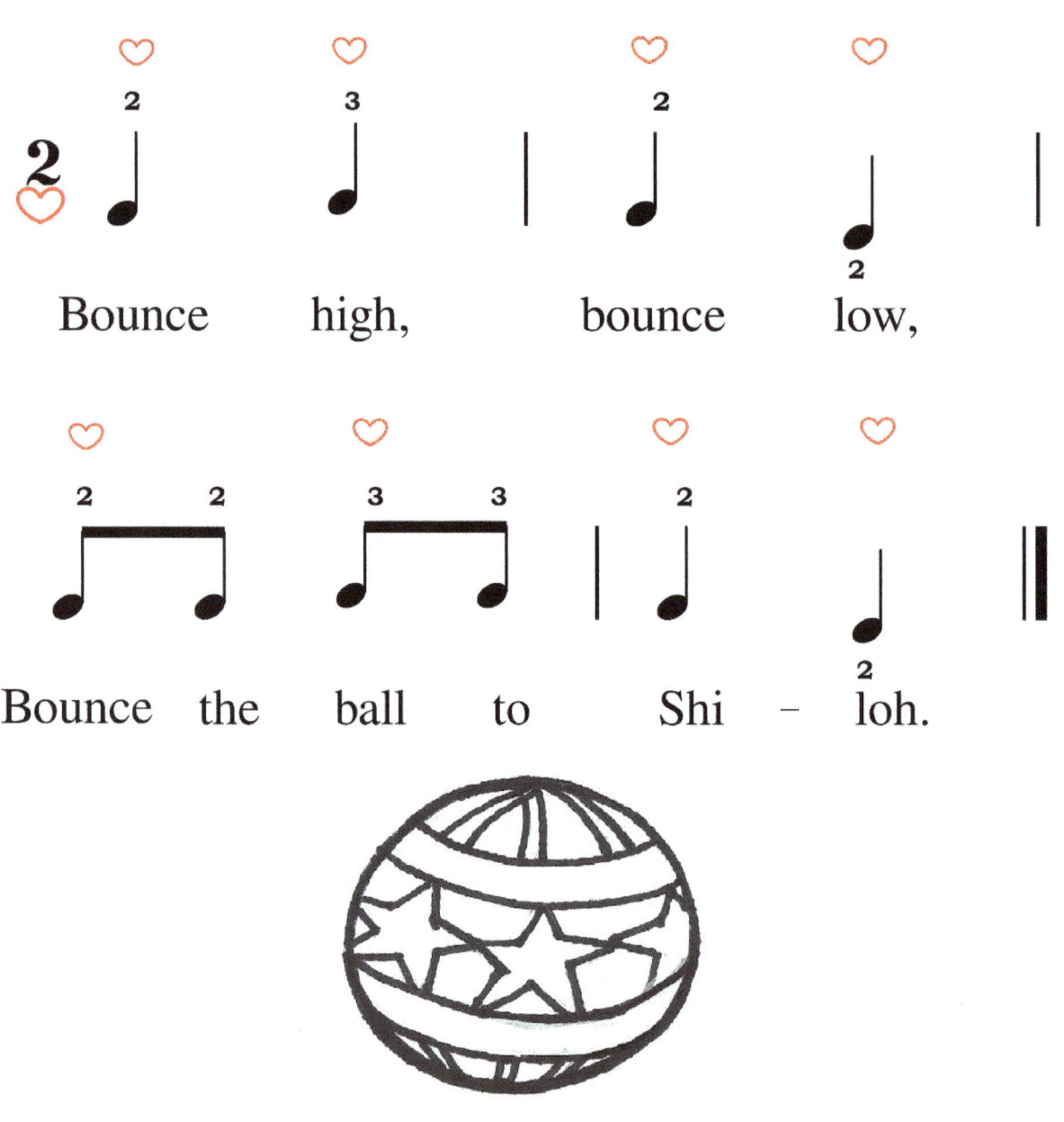

Resource Guide

PLAINSIES, CLAPSIES

Plain-sies, clap-sies, twirl a-round to back-sies. Right hand,

left hand, Toss it high, toss it low, Touch your knee,

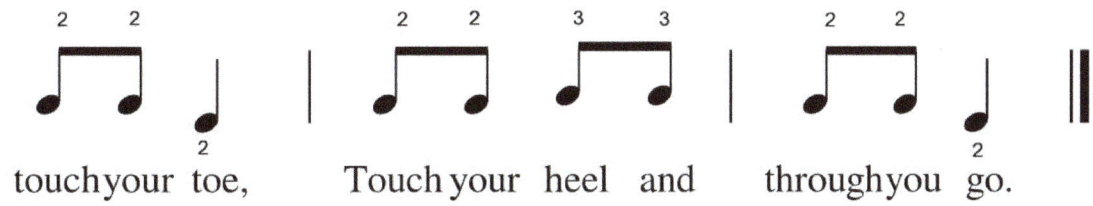

touch your toe, Touch your heel and through you go.

LUCY LOCKET

Luc - y Loc - ket lost her poc - ket,

Kit - ty Fish - er found it. Not a pen - ny

was there in it, on - ly rib-bon 'round it.

www.ingramcontent.com/pod-product-compliance
Lightning Source LLC
Chambersburg PA
CBHW042037100526
44587CB00030B/4458

Girls Can Journal, Too

A Journal For Girls To Express Their Feelings

Girls Can Journal, Too

Copyright 2020 TwentyEighth Publishing
Written By Wendy Ball Bridgeman

All rights reserved. No part of this book may be used or reproduced in any manner whatsoever without the prior written permission of the author.